My quiet place

Birds

Aleksandra Mršić

Copyright © 2023 AleksandraMršić
All rights reserved.
ISBN:9798359744843

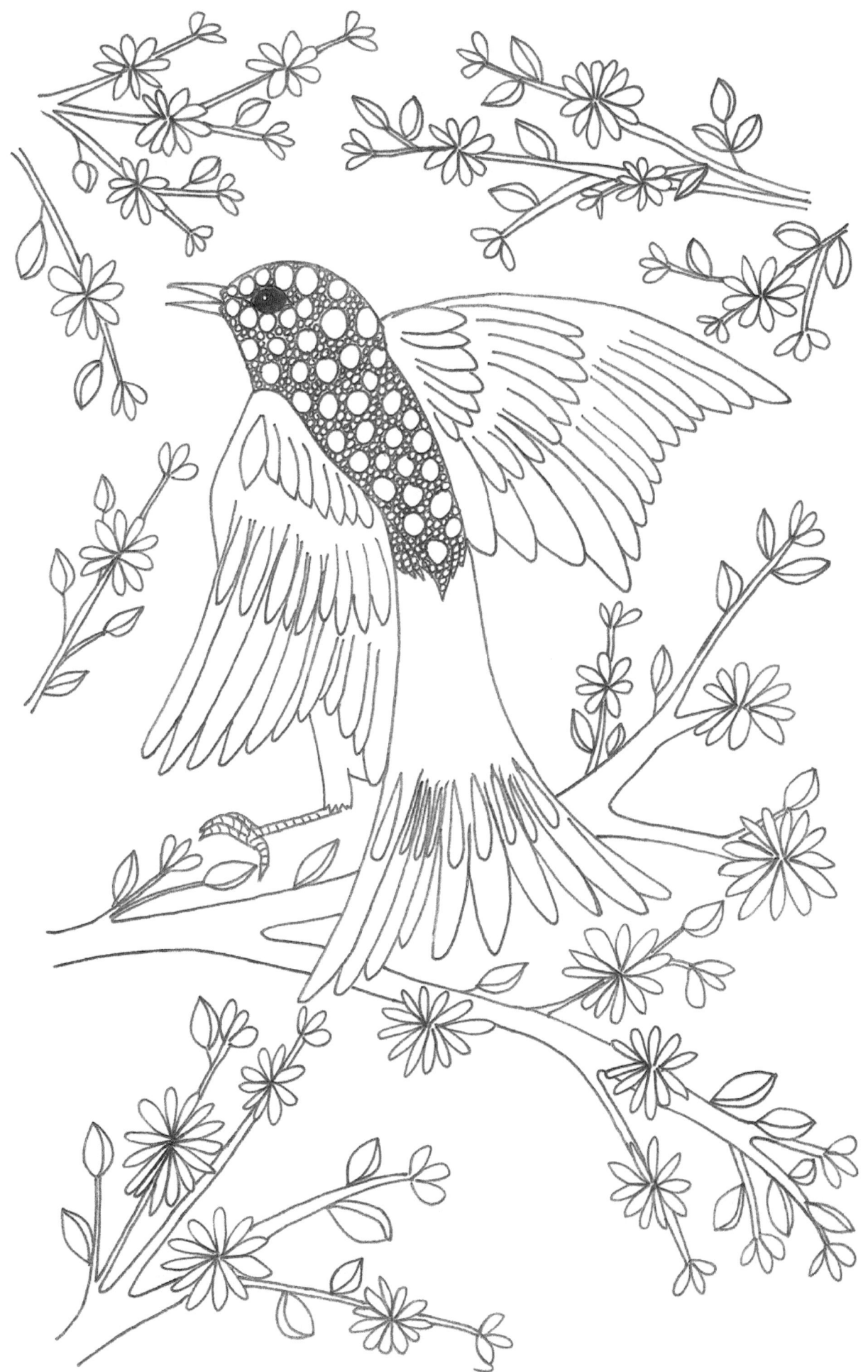

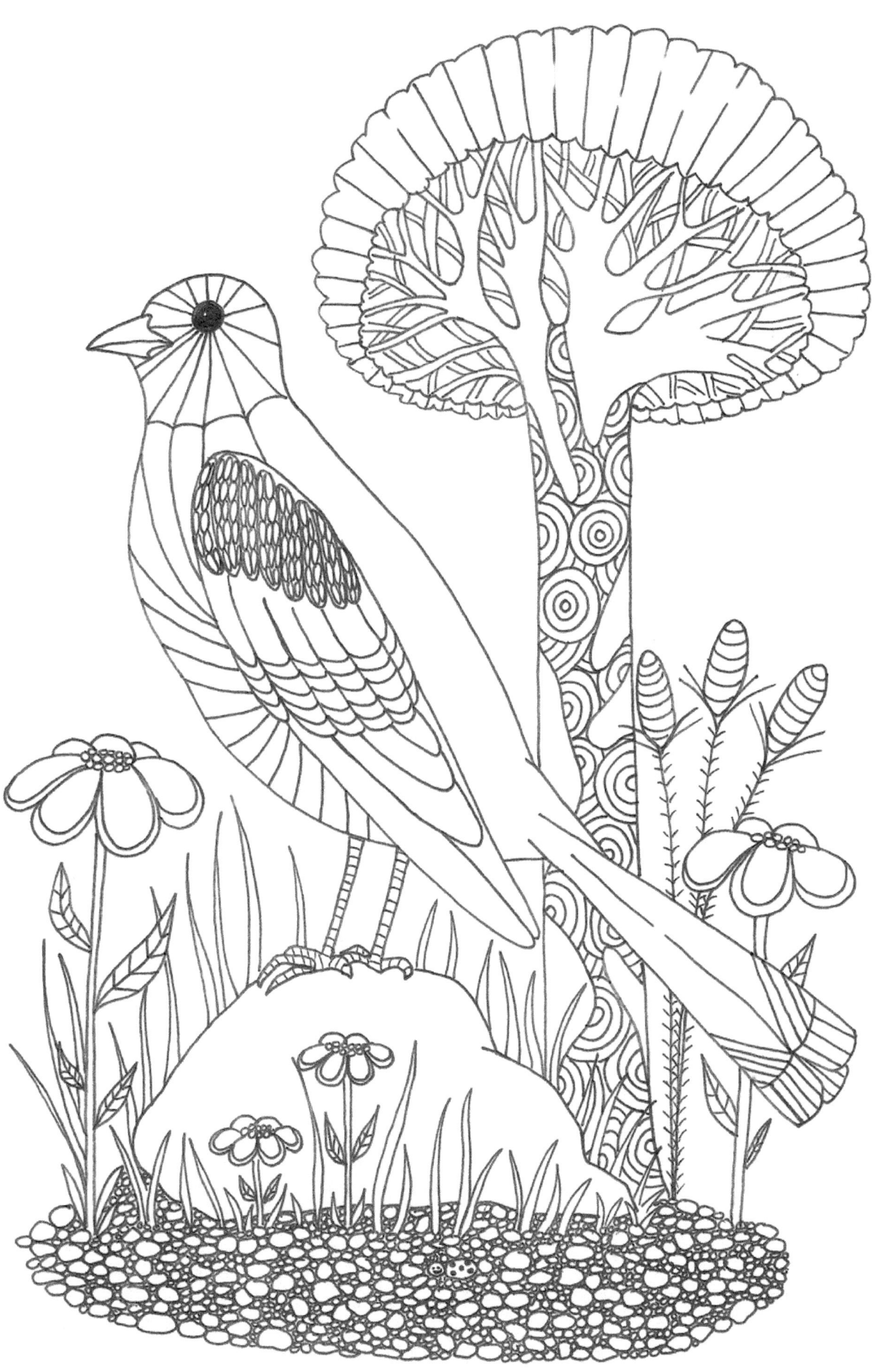

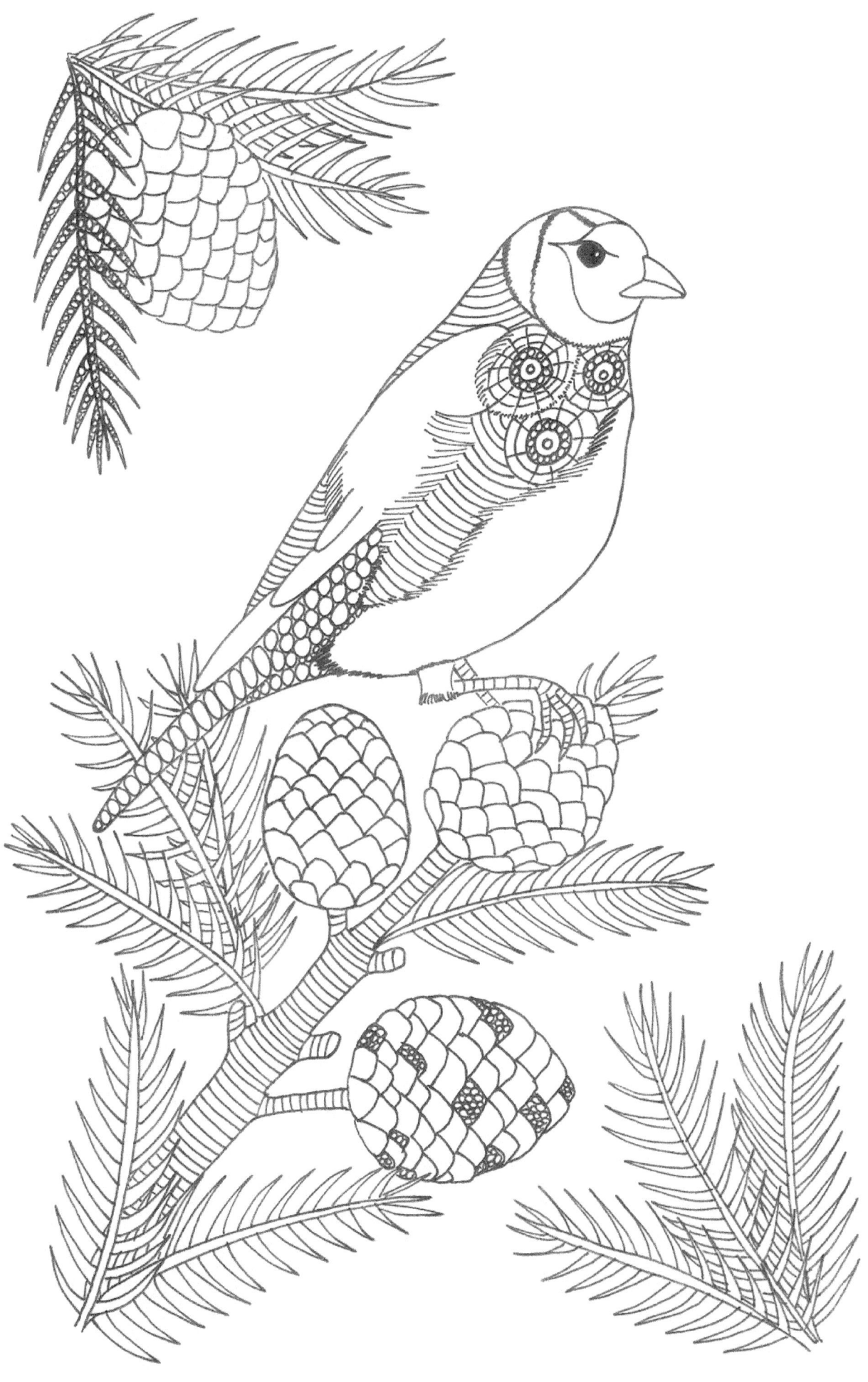

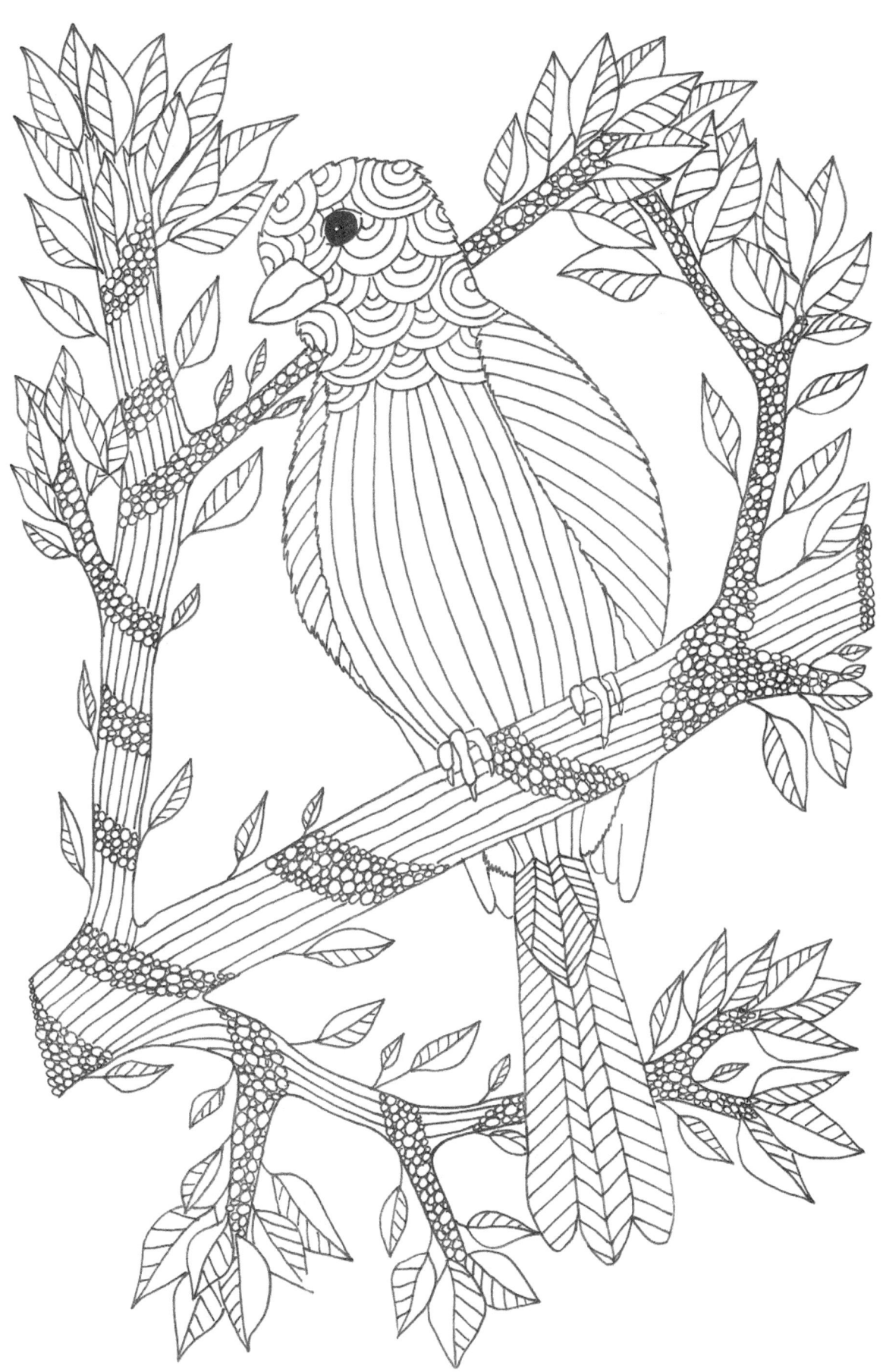

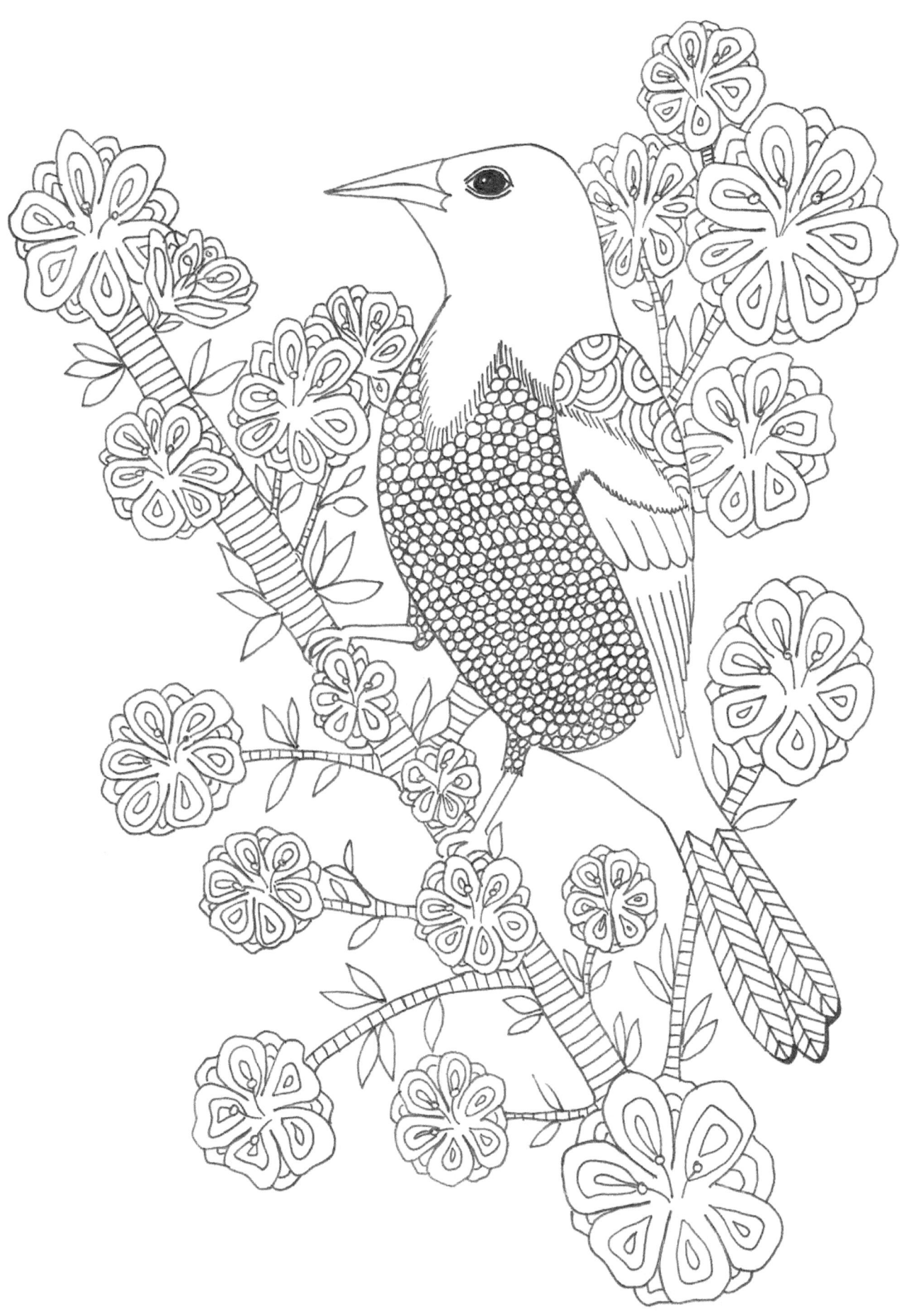

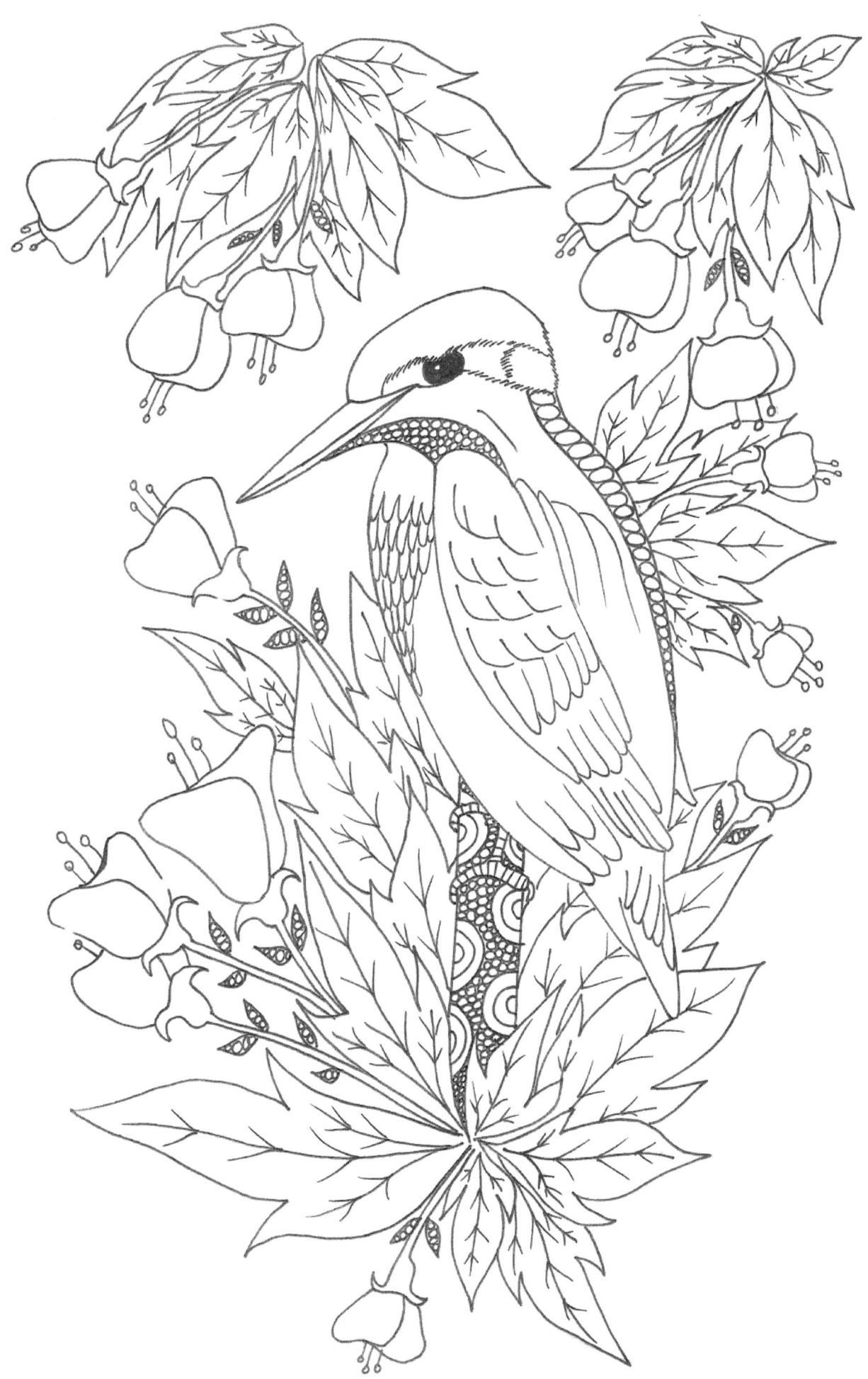

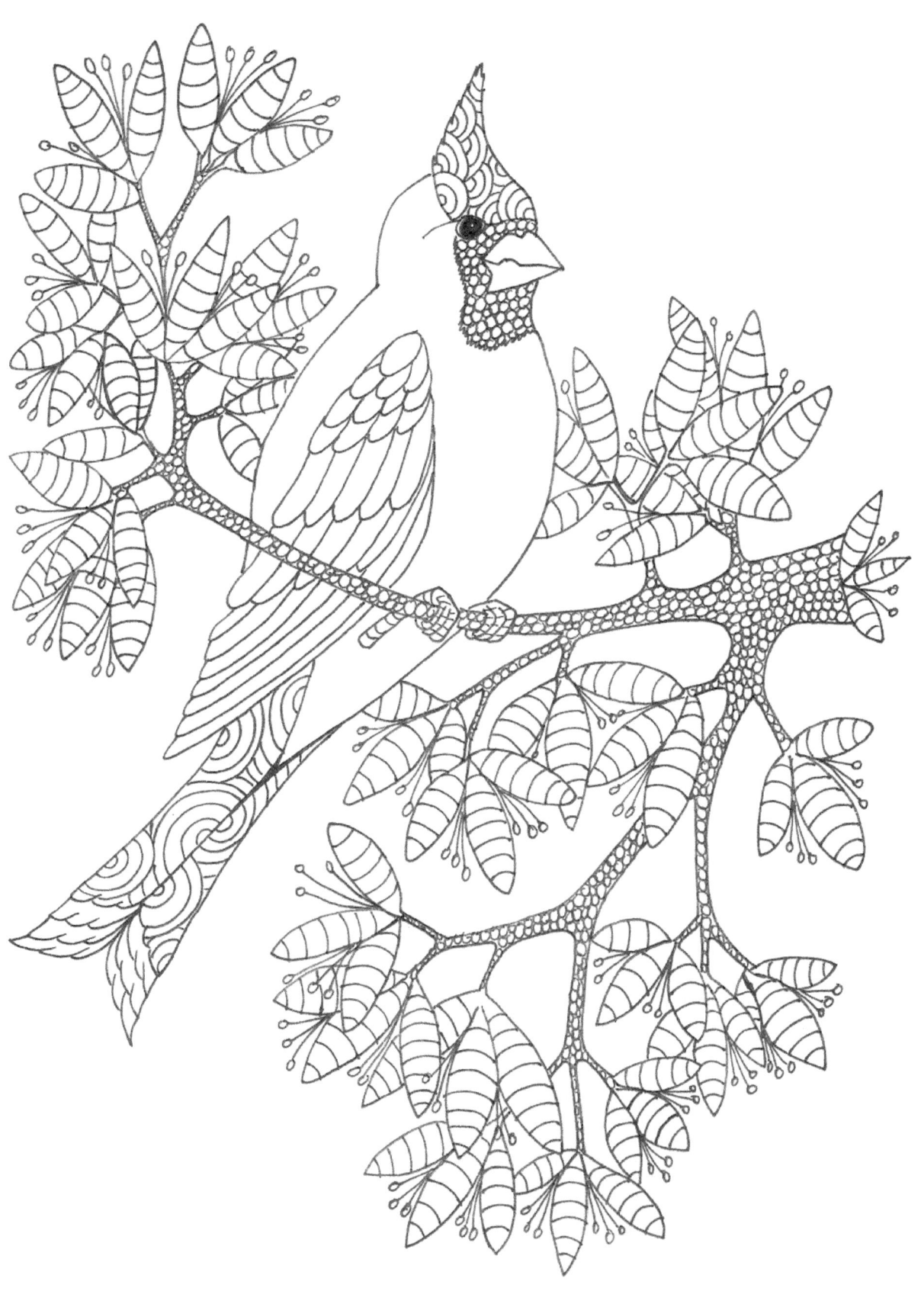

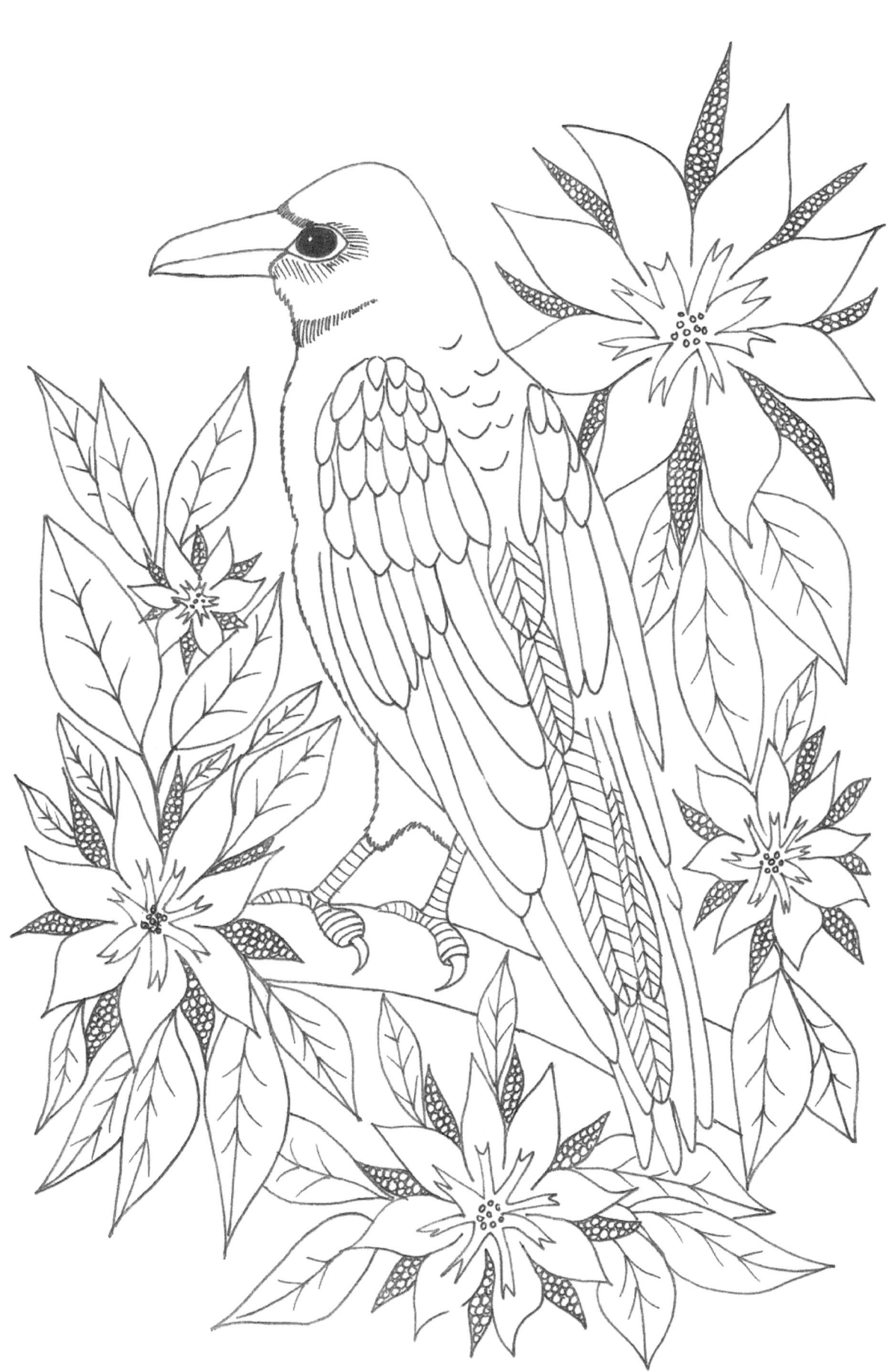

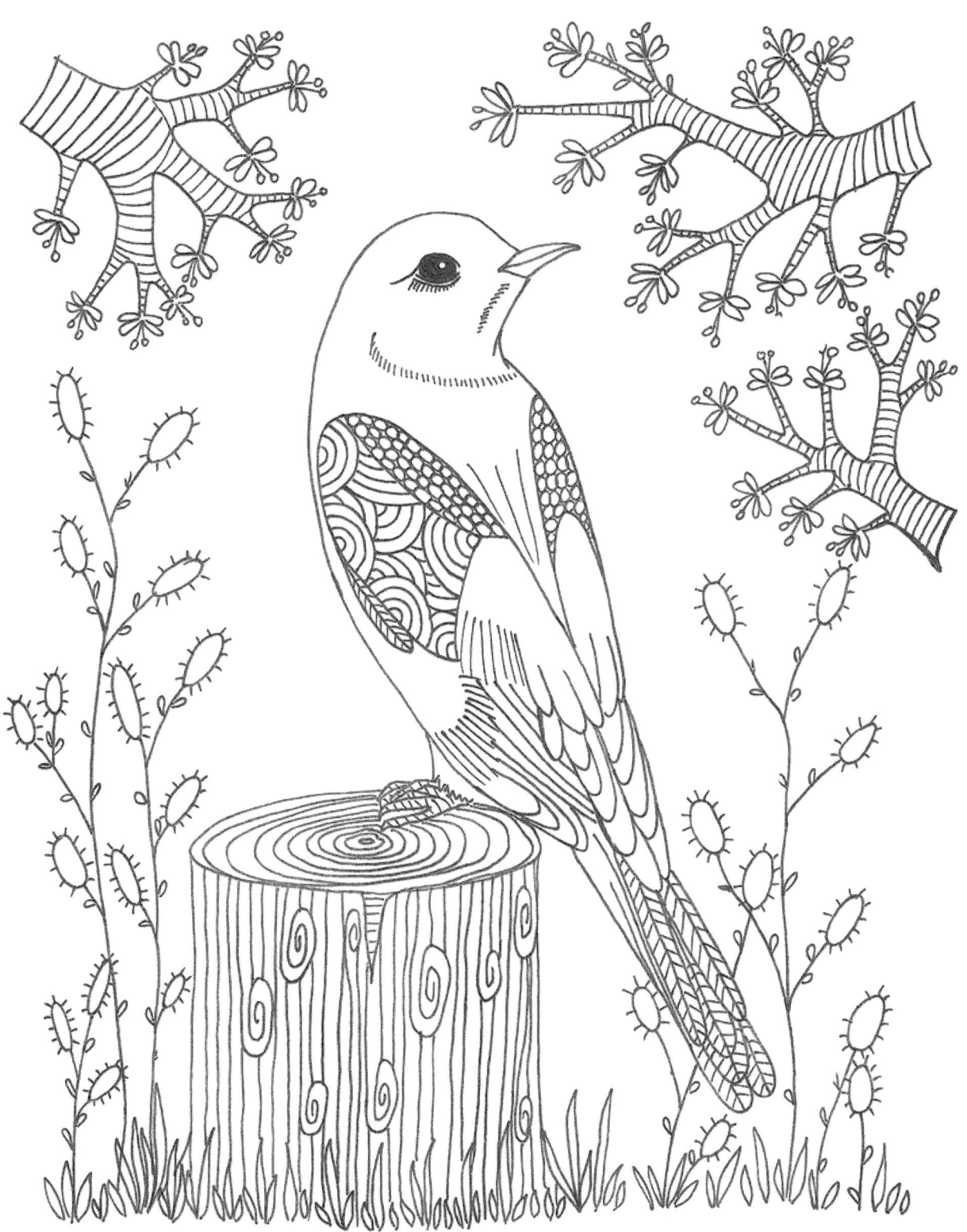

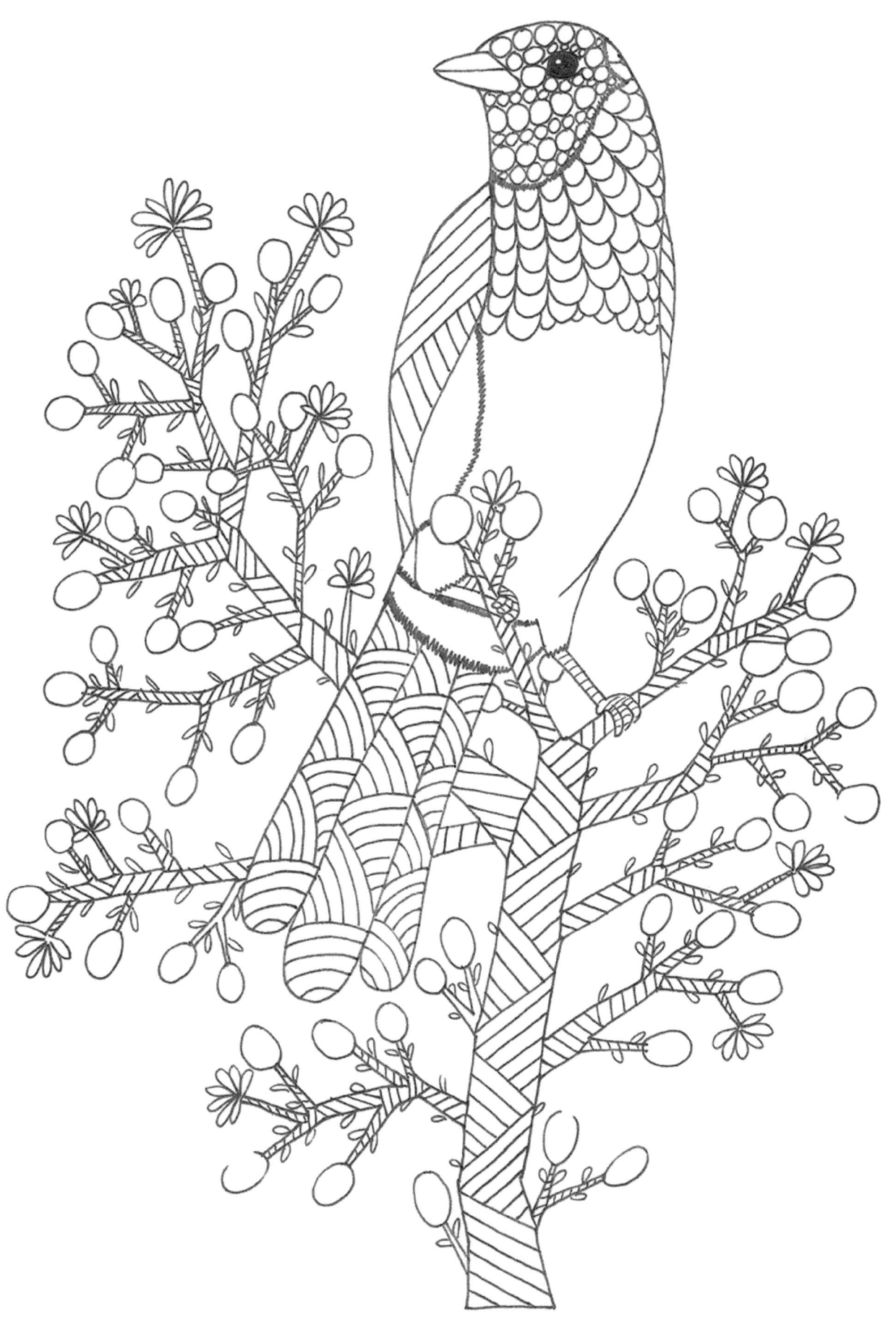

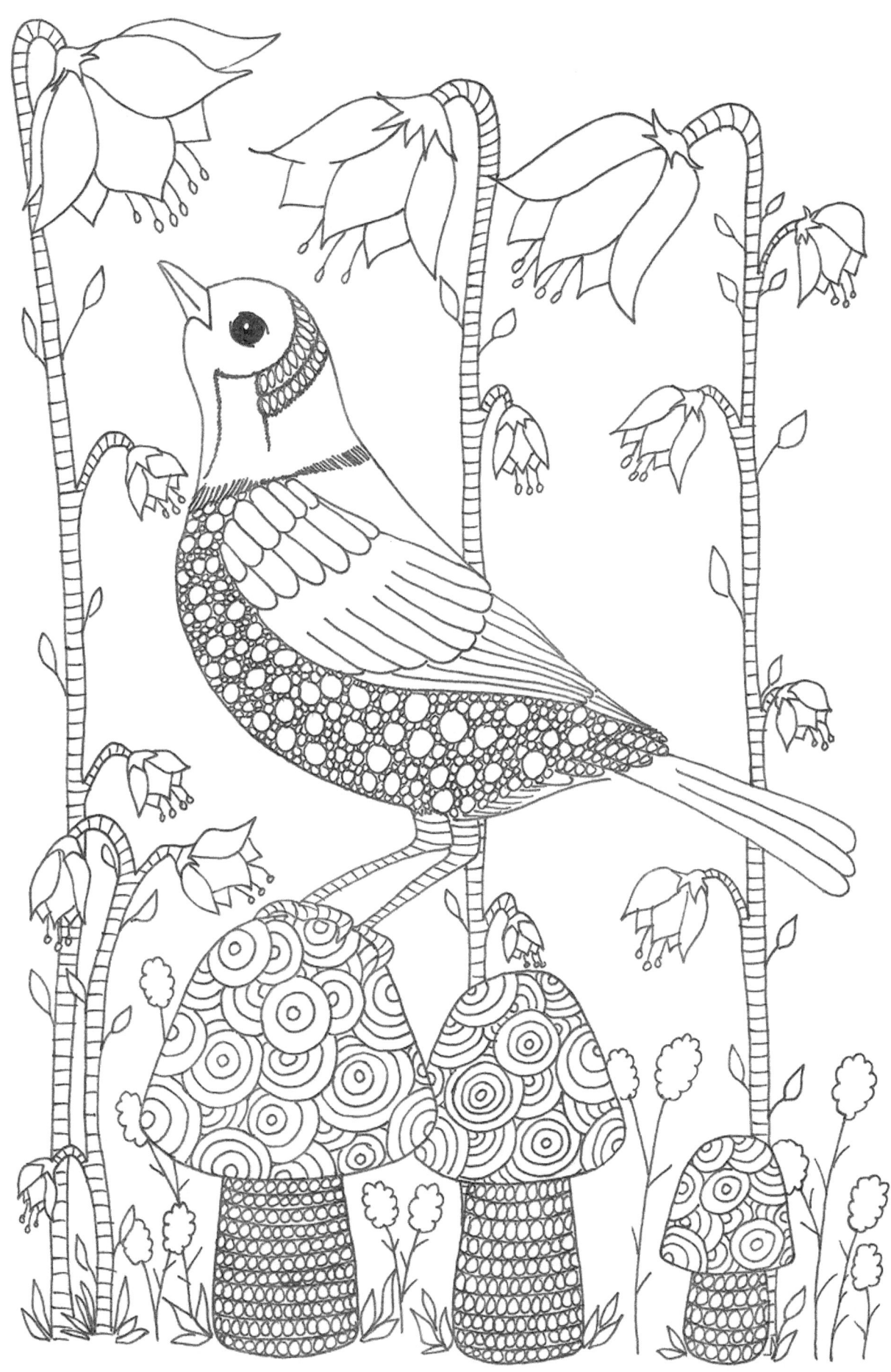

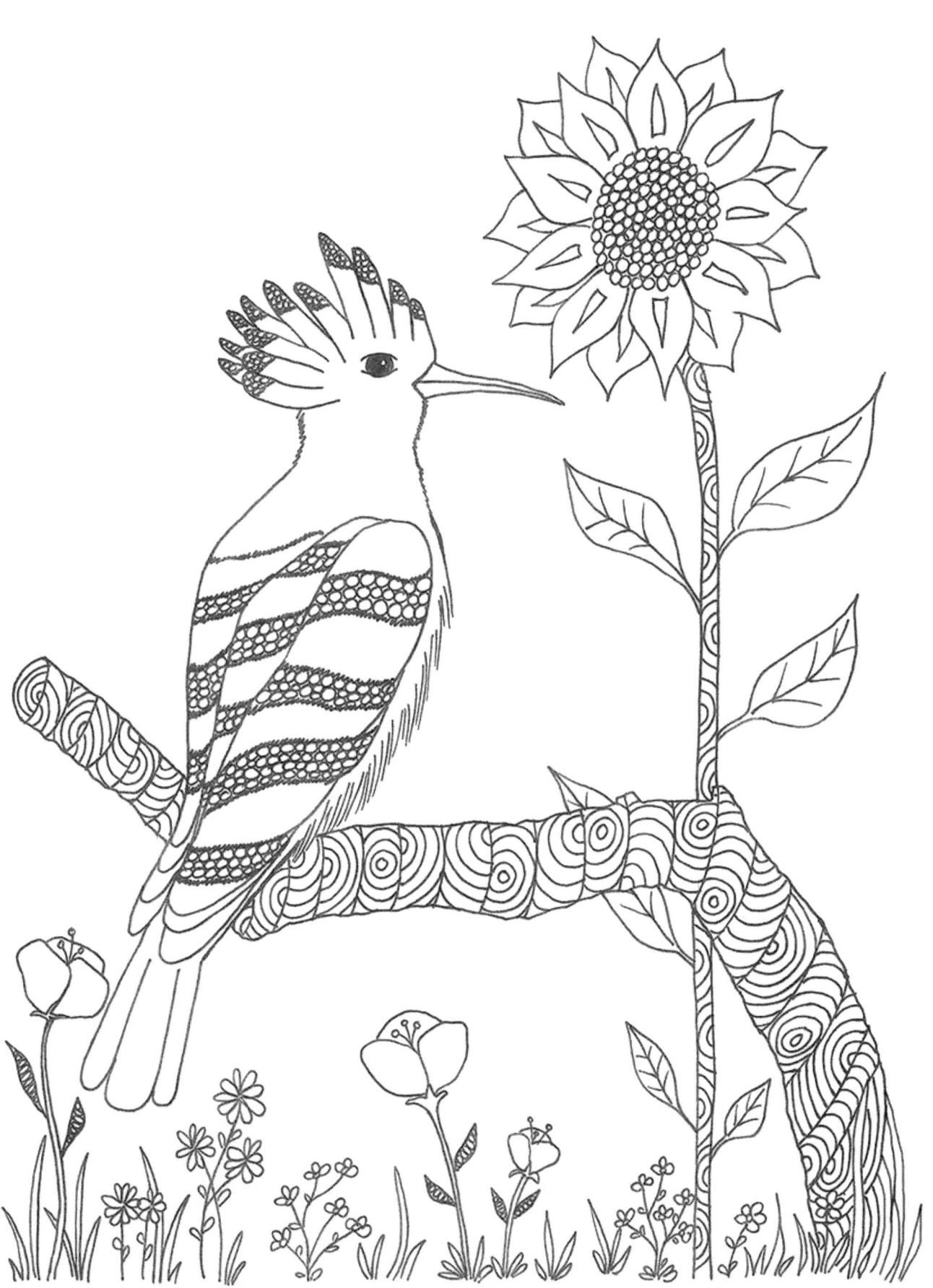

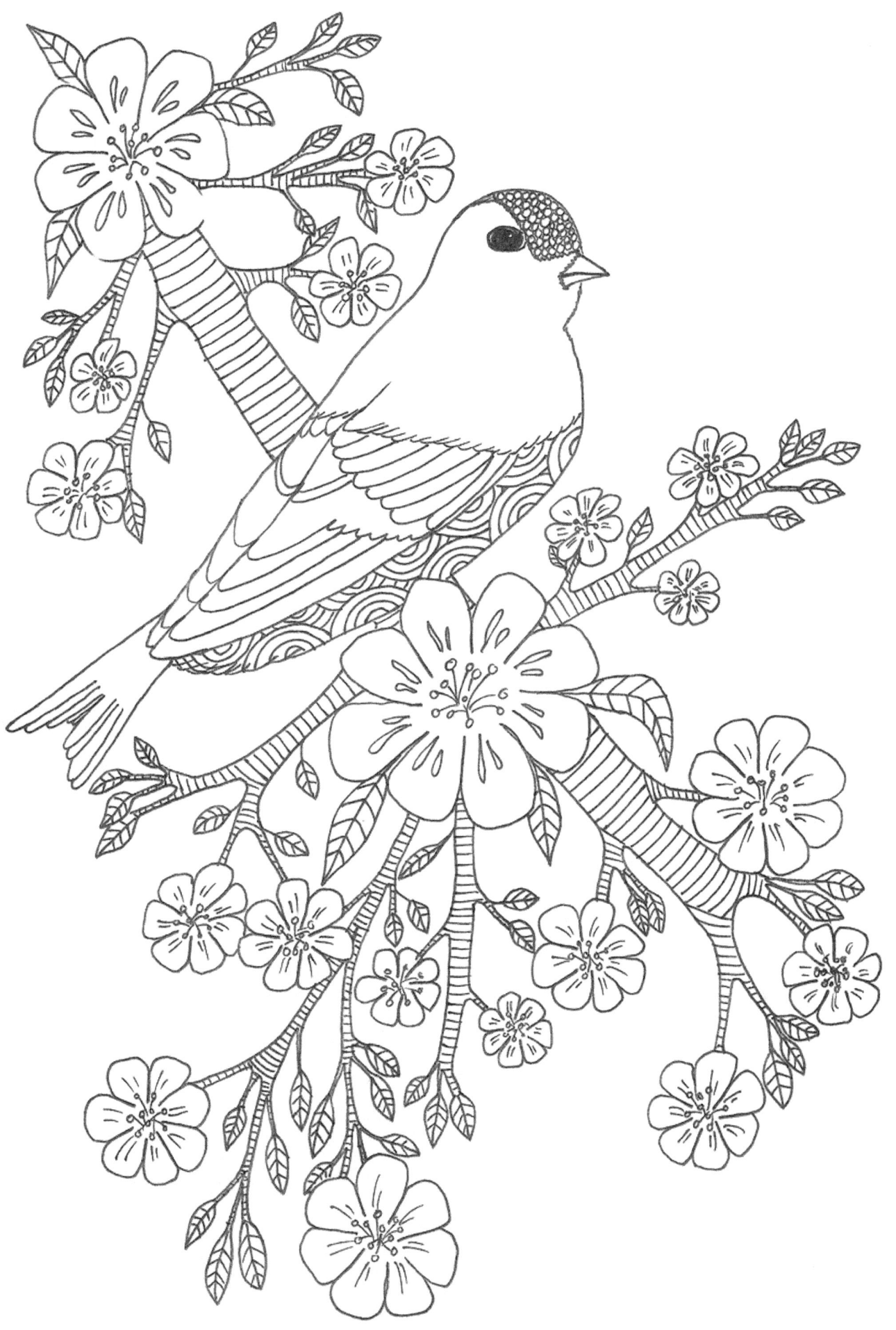

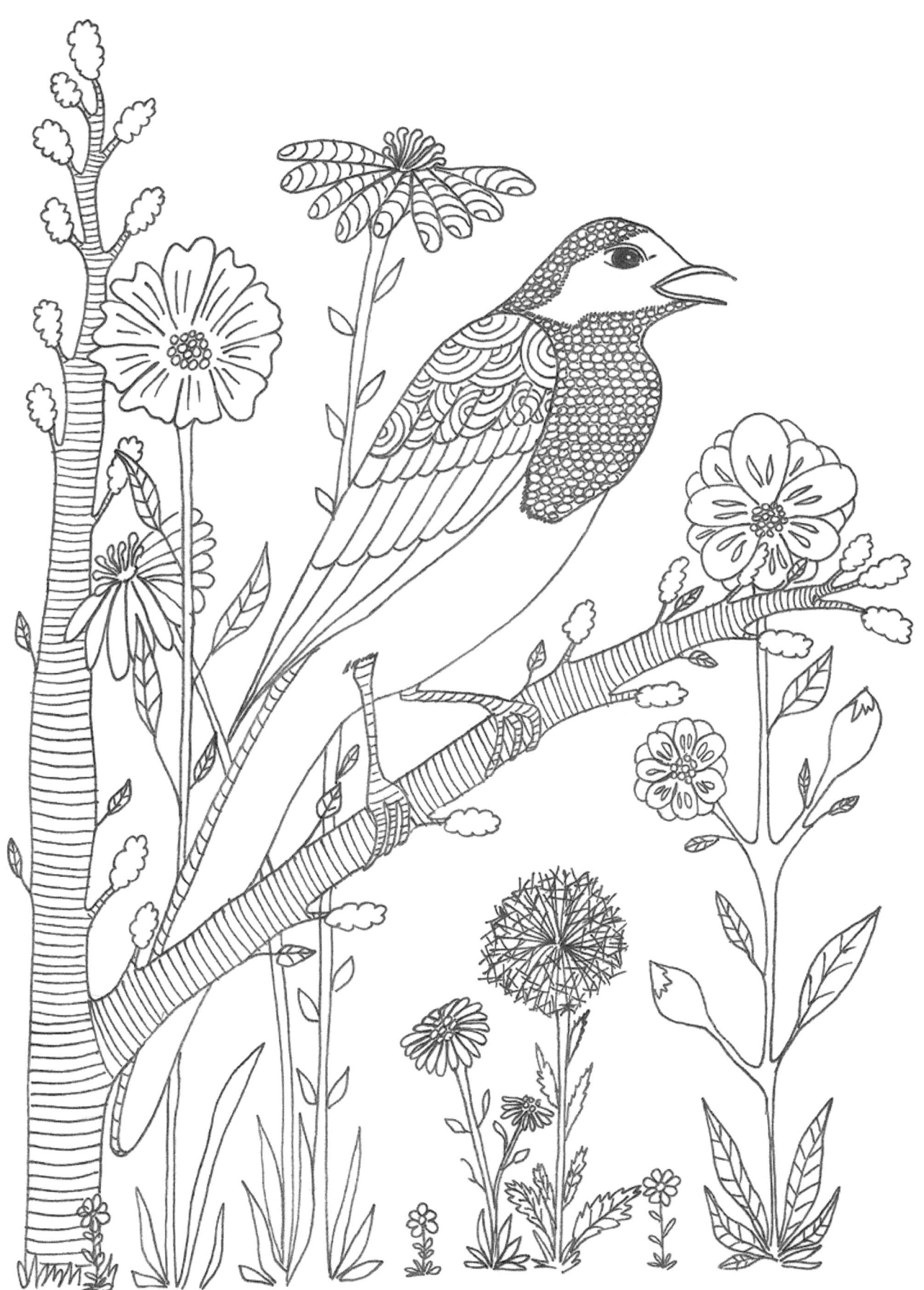

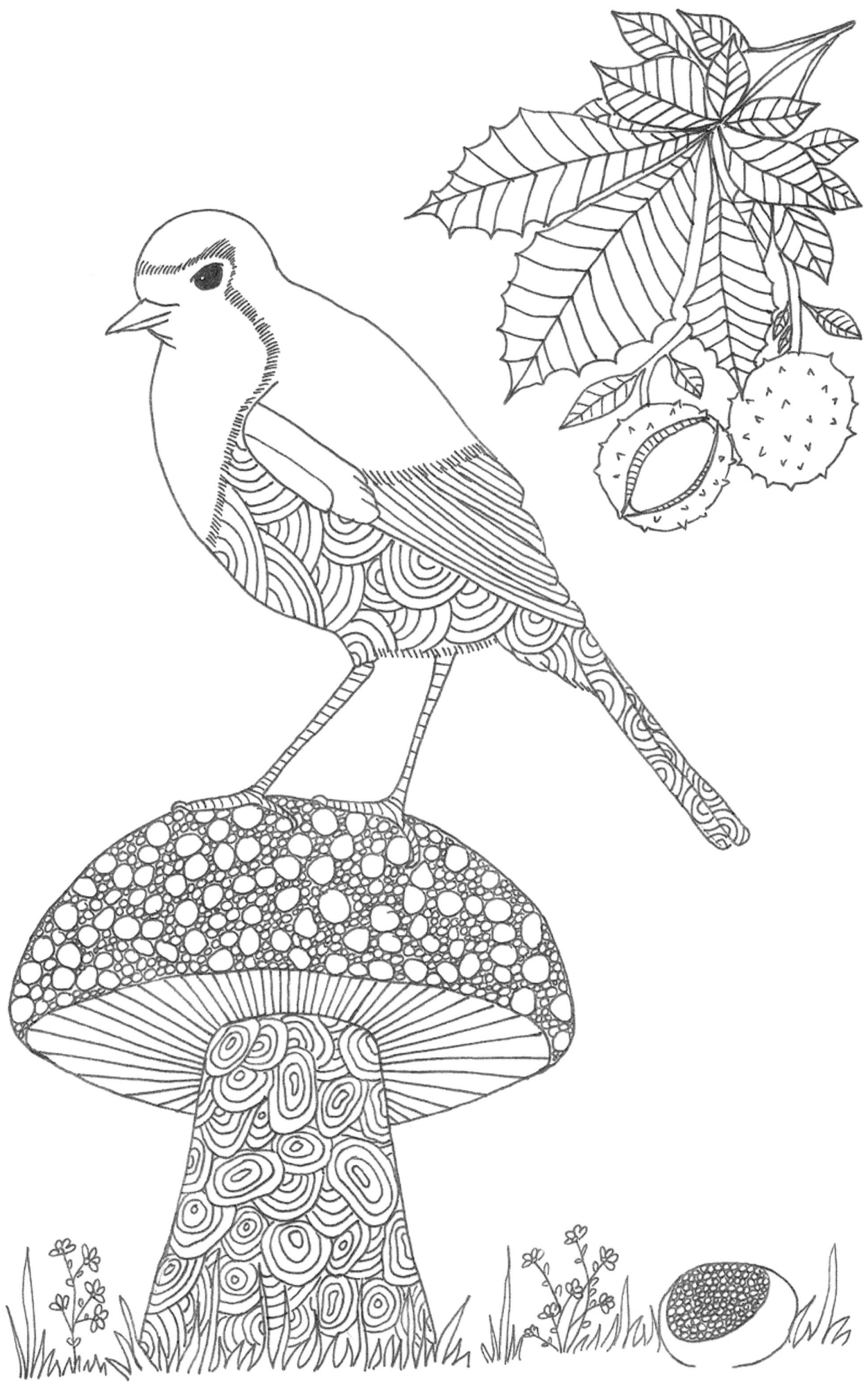

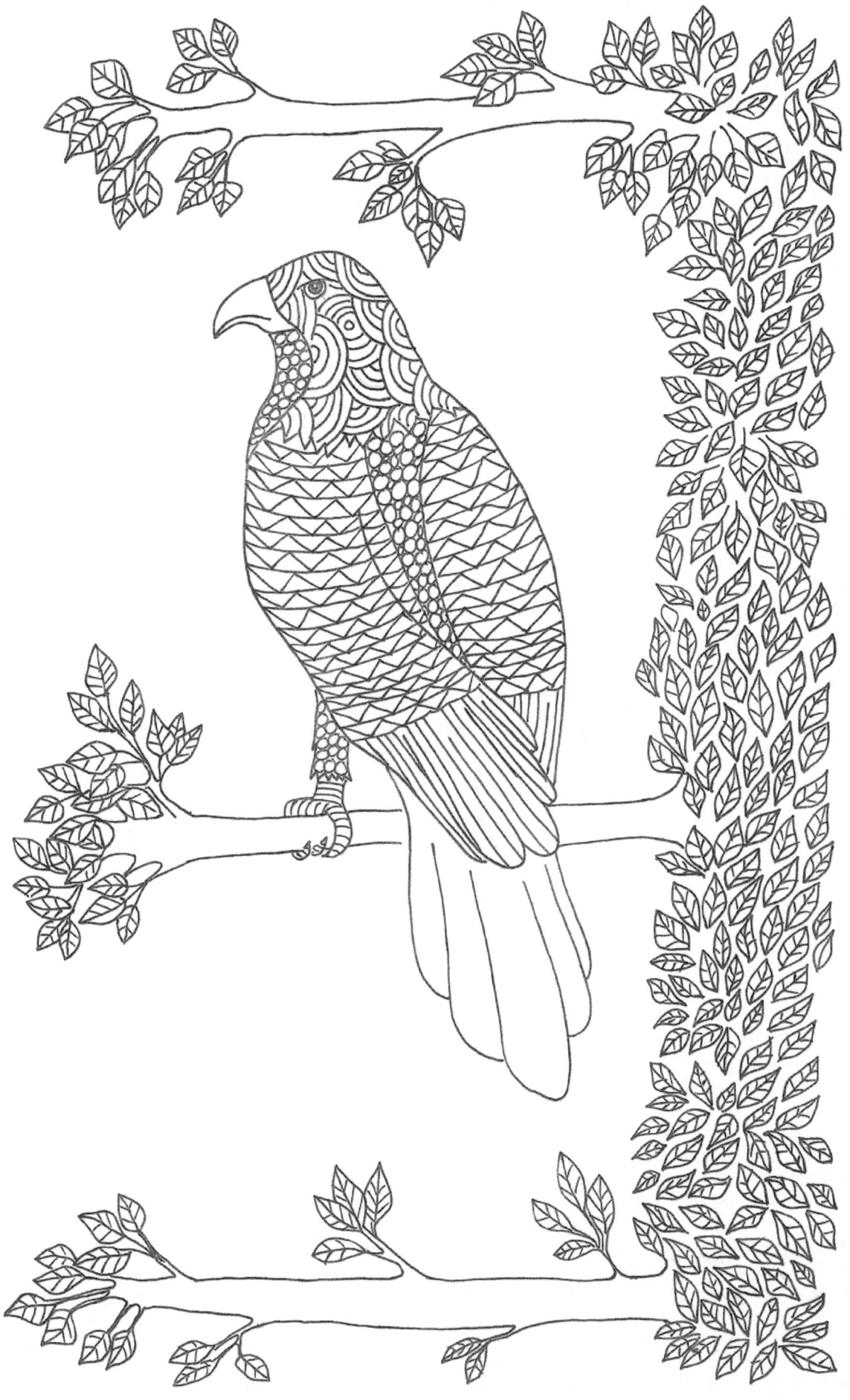

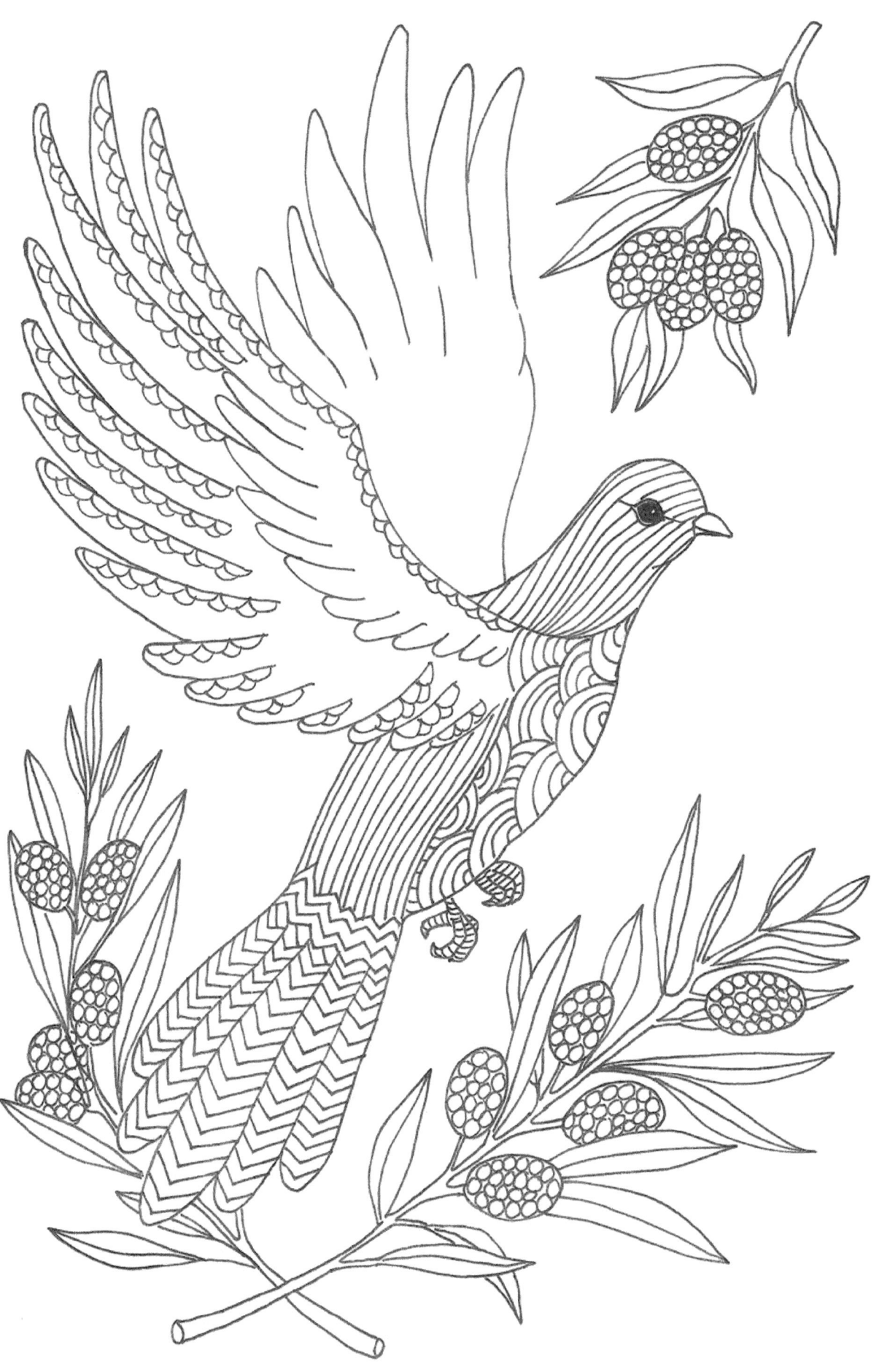

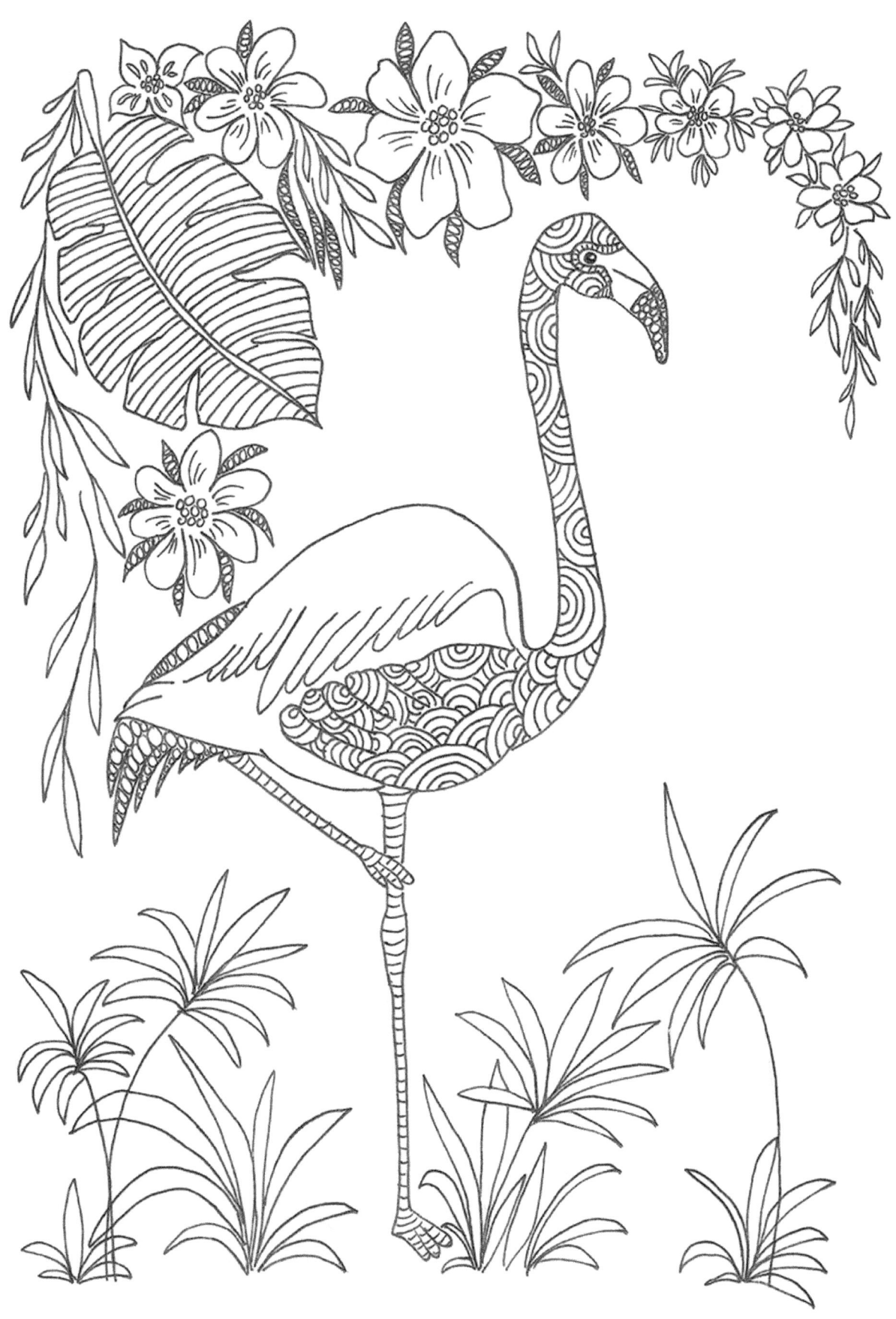

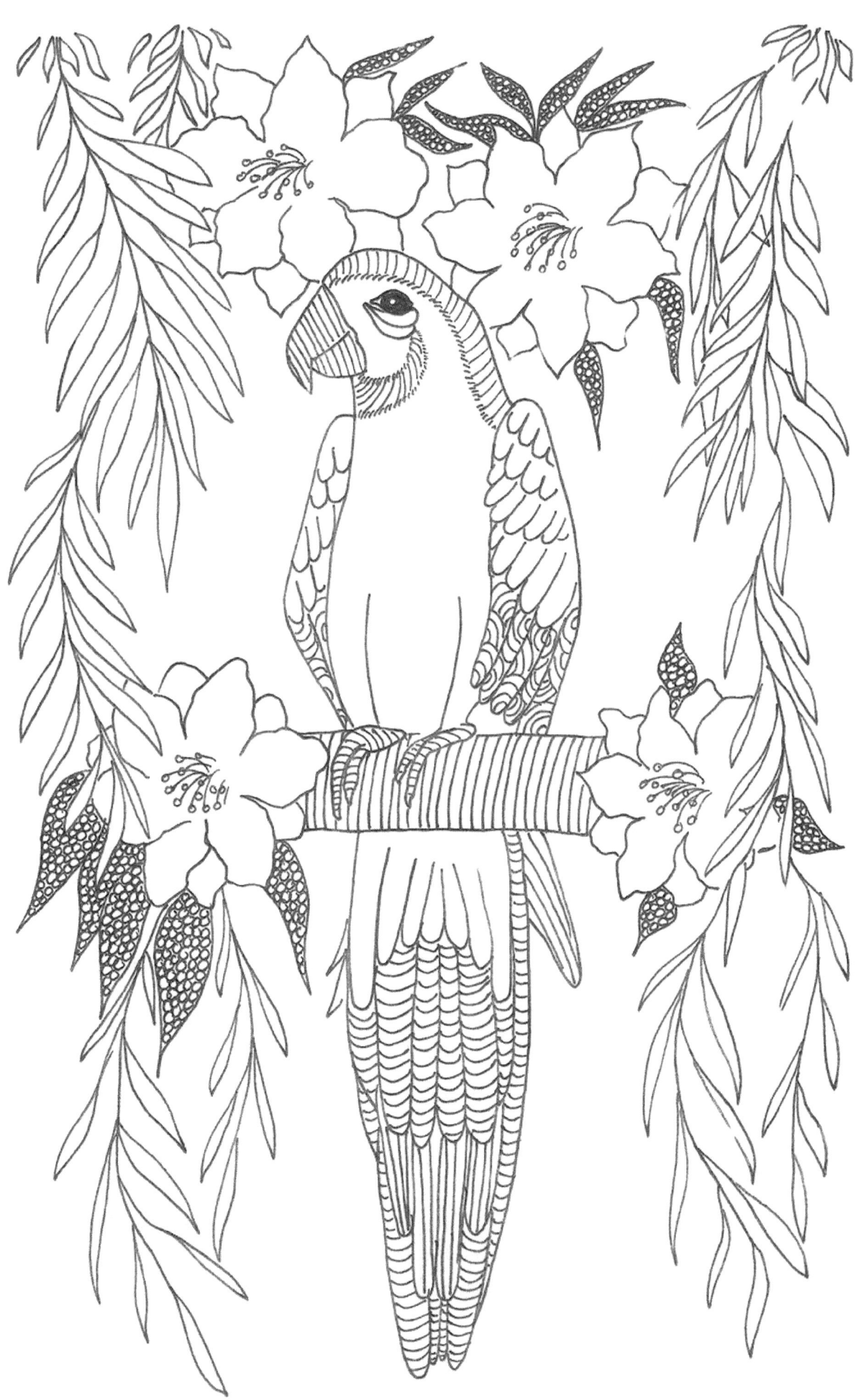

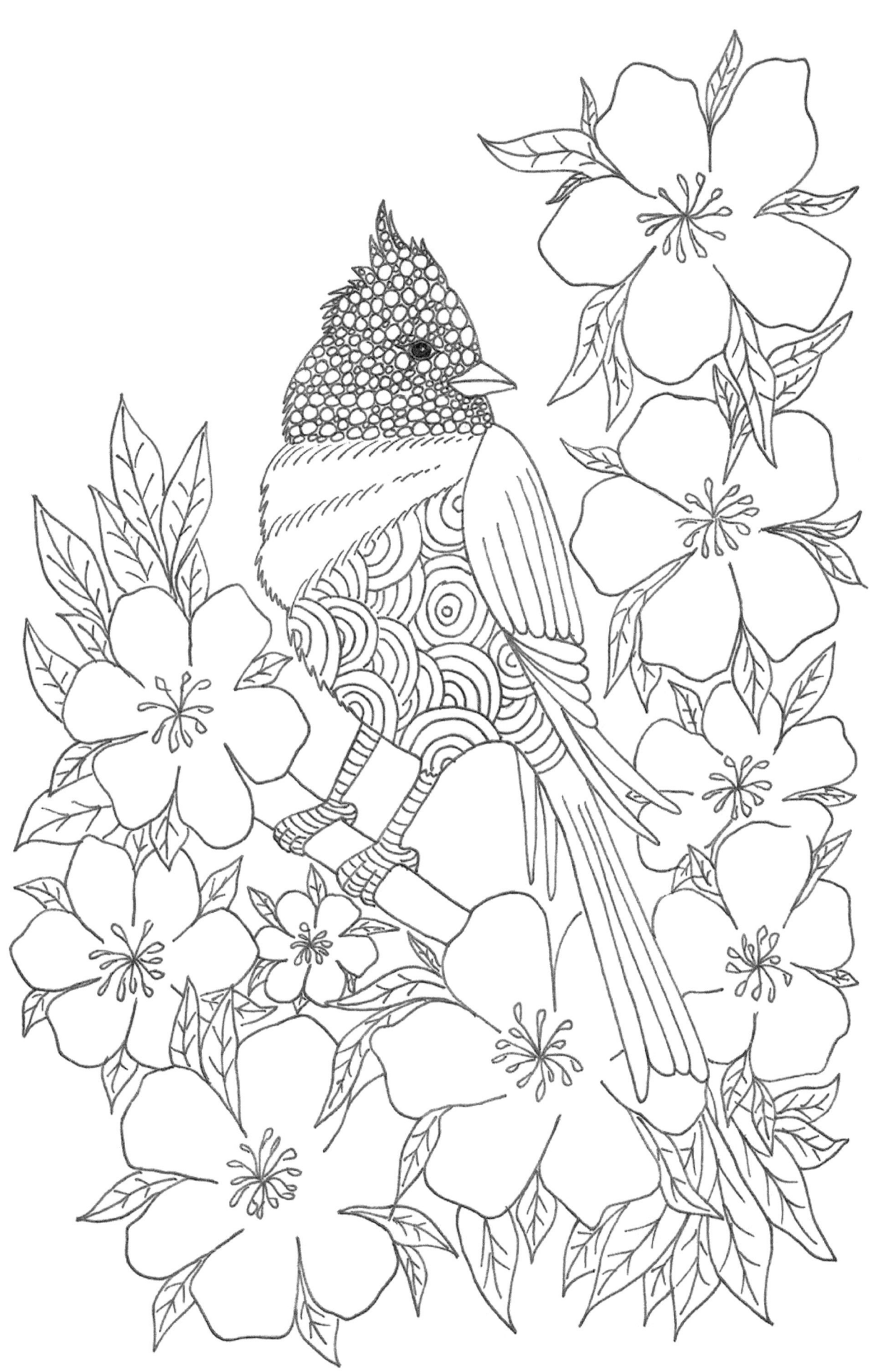

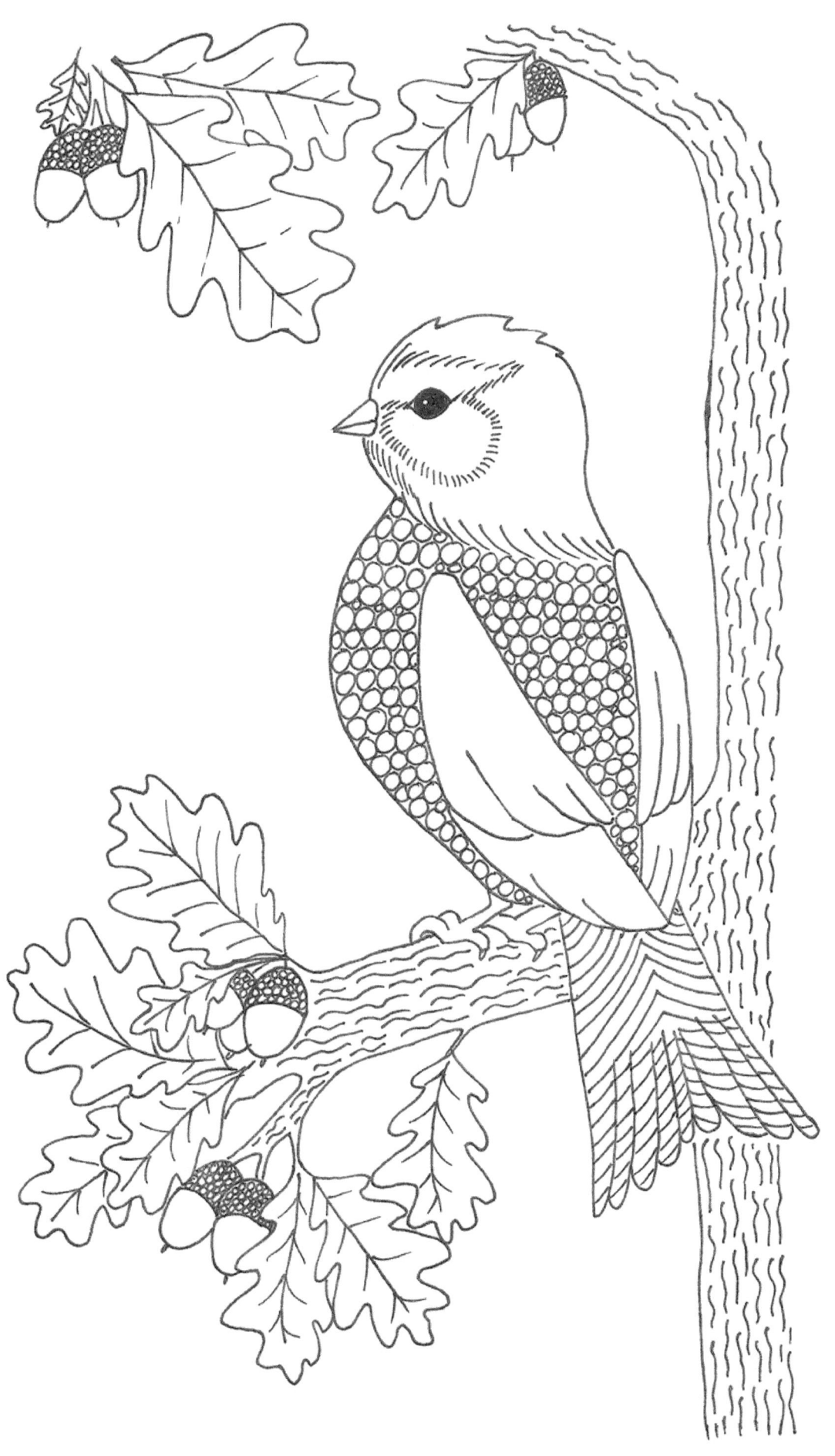

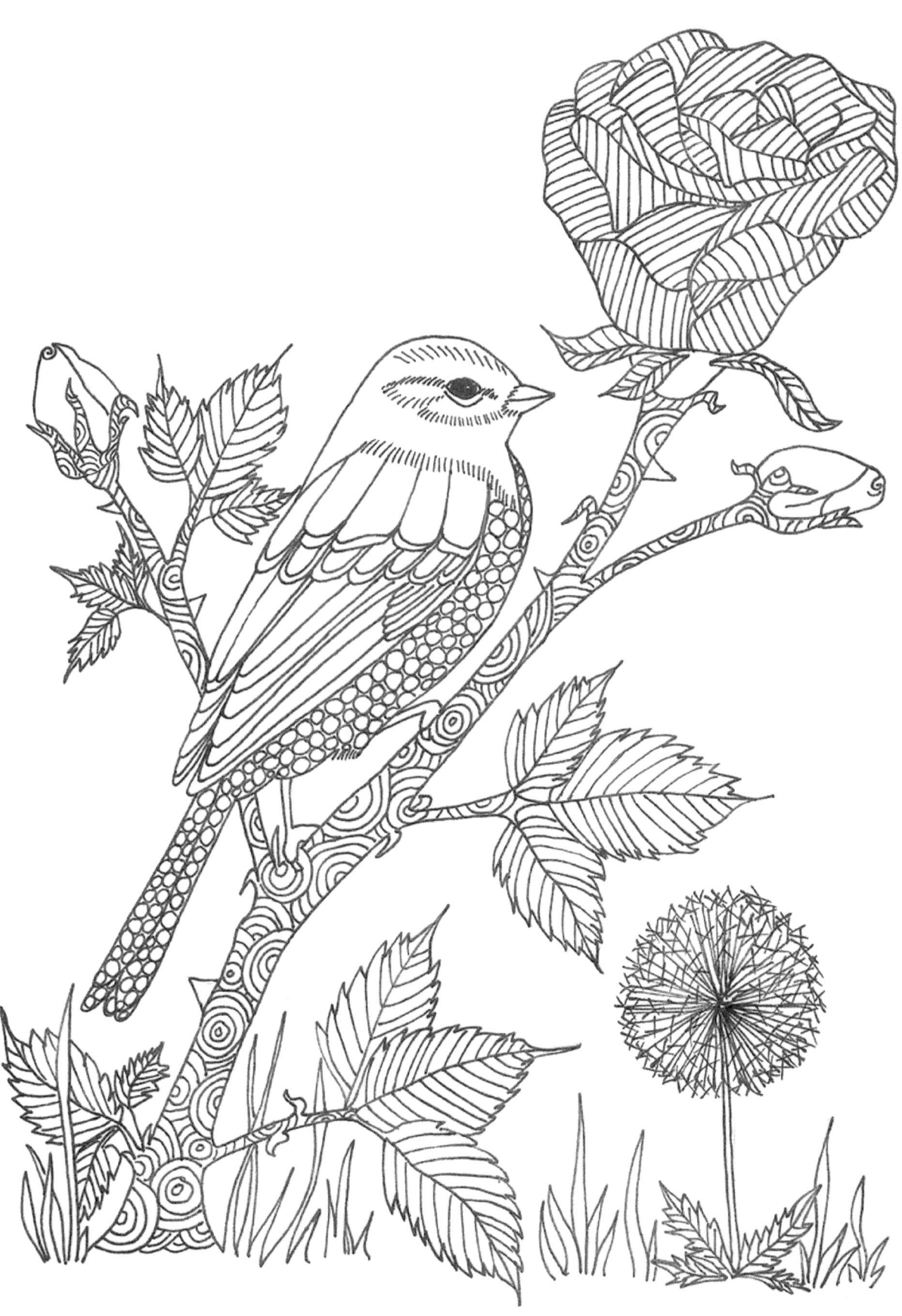

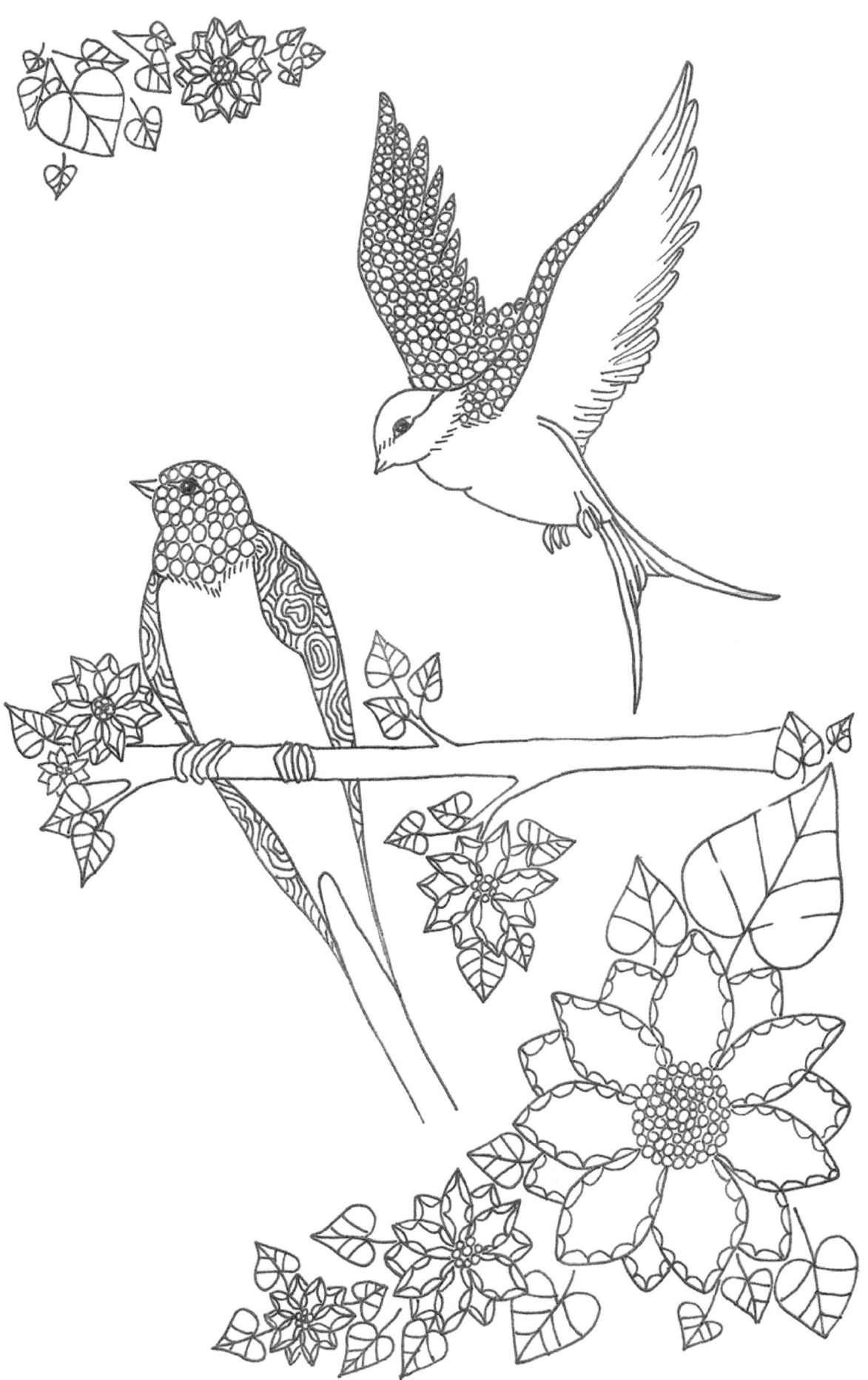

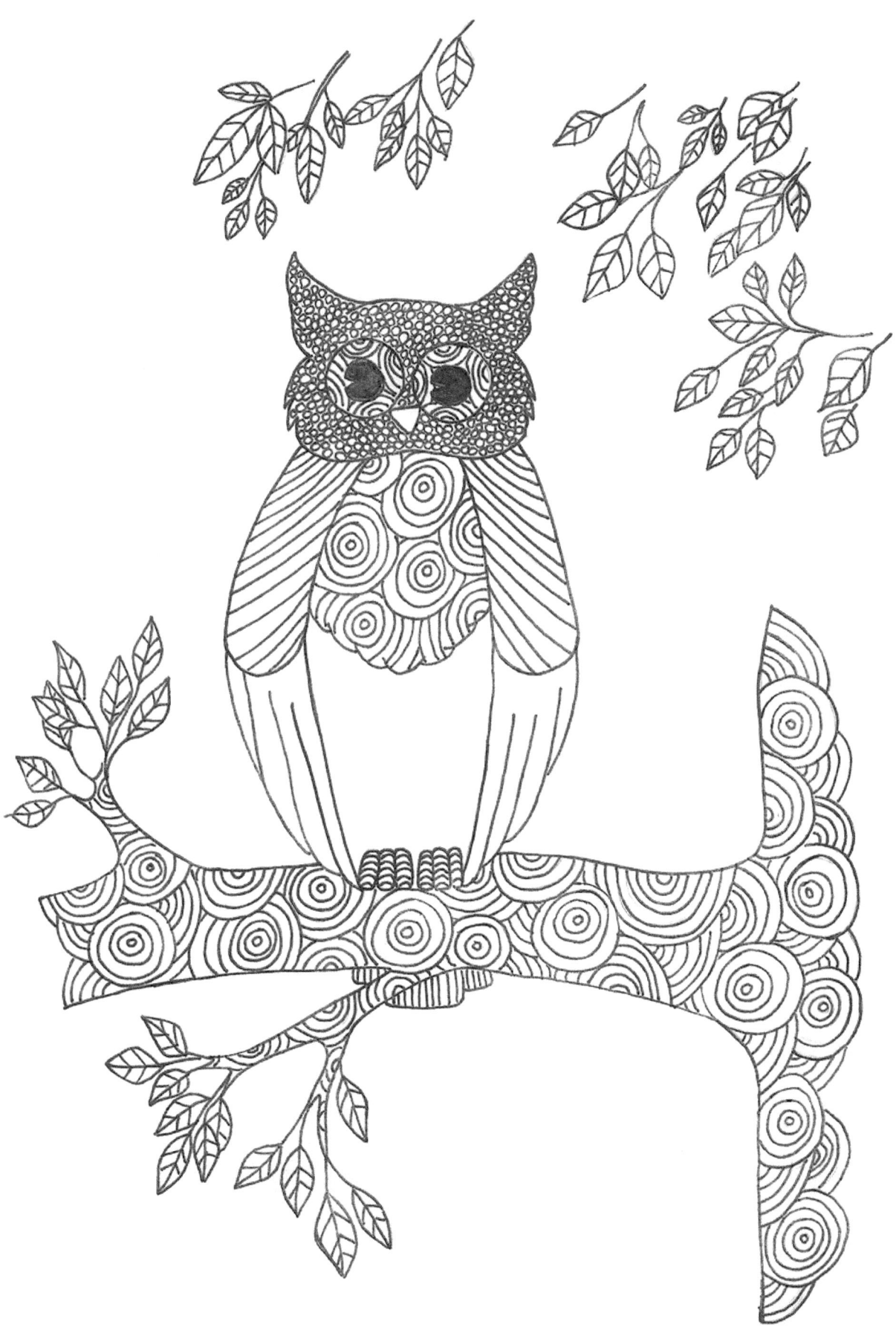

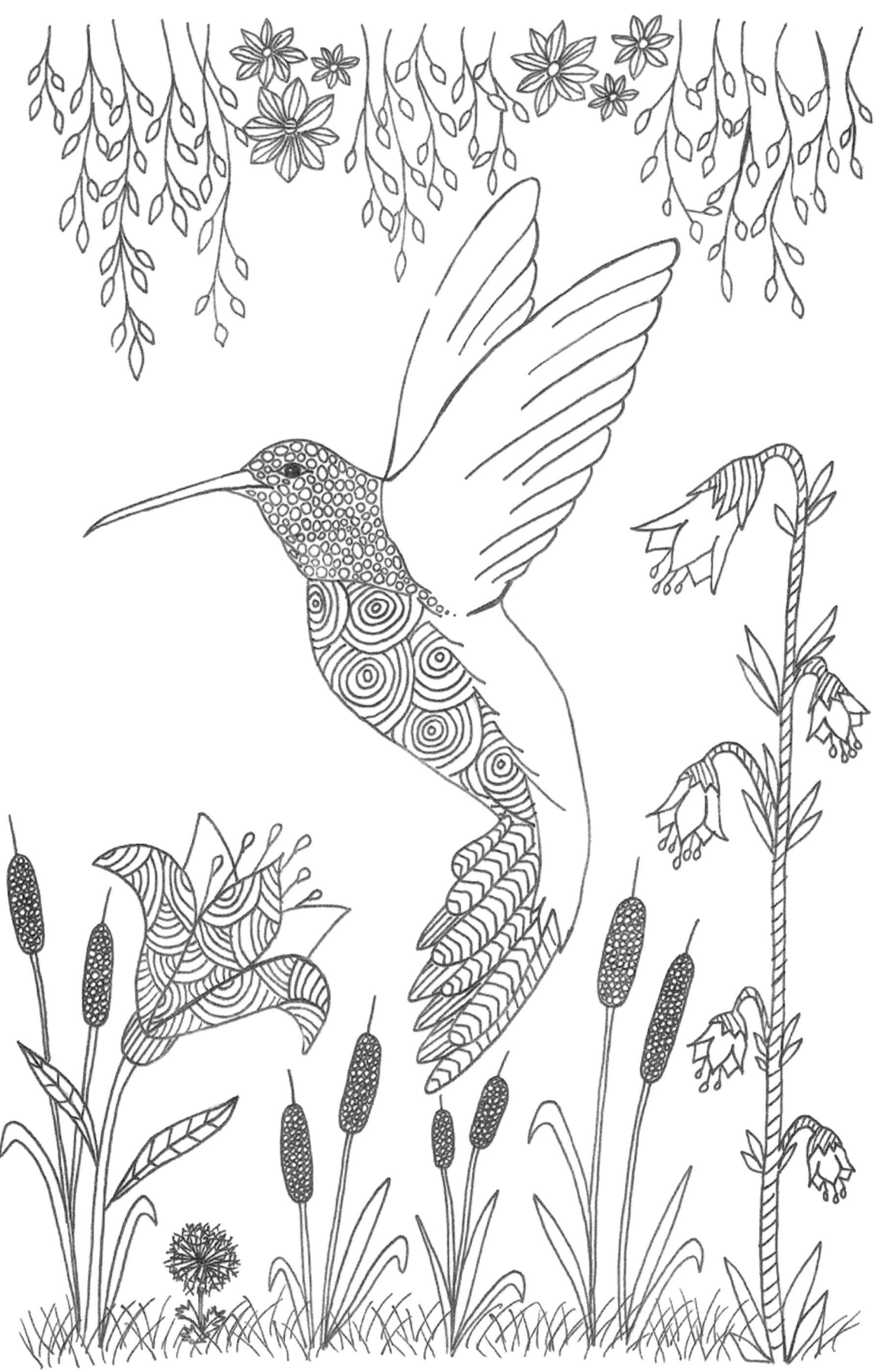

www.ingramcontent.com/pod-product-compliance
Lightning Source LLC
Chambersburg PA
CBHW080443220526

45465CB00007B/2749